PRODUCTION COST FUNCTION FOR BANKNOTE PRINTING INDUSTRY

Editor: Dr. Hitesh Gupta

Journal: International Journal of Management & Social Sciences (IJMSS)

Author: N. Krishnaswamy

Affiliation: PhD Scholar, Indira Gandhi National Open University, New Delhi, India.

Abstract

Banknote printing industry has undergone major structural changes in the past decade. This has been explored in this study with special focus to its performance. This study has taken up task of identifying the variables involved in its production cost. It has attempted proposing a production cost function for evaluating its production performance. The variables considered include population of the country, currency in circulation, per capita income, number of denominations produced and circulating in the economy, average number of security features, average size of the banknotes and the method used by the central bank to produce banknotes.

Keywords: Production cost function, Banknote, Printing, Printing industry, Currency, Monopsony.

1. INTRODUCTION

The National Industrial Classification called Standard Industrial Classification (SIC) – NIC-2008 code 18114: Printing of Bank notes, Currency notes which classifies the Banknote Printing Industry in India.[11] The cost of banknote production has a major bearing on the monetary economy due to the fact that the volume of production is very high. This paper examines the role of different variables those are affecting cost of banknotes in India.

The study seeks to identify the various components of the banknotes and its production methods and derive a cost function through its key variables in the banknote production cost function and their relative importance in banknote printing for the period of ten years from 2000 to 2010.

India is producing more banknotes than each previous year. Its production and supply of banknotes has increased from 8657 million banknote pieces in 2001 to 16416 million pieces in 2010, which is a growth of 189.63 percent.[40] Cost of production of banknotes in India is one of the lowest in the world. Availability of banknotes per person is Rs. 7196.653 by value, which is one of the lowest in the world.[41]

1.1. Banknote Printing Industry

- **Banknote** - To sustain public confidence in a circulating currency, banknotes must contain features that the public can use to readily judge their authenticity and determine the notes' denominations. Monetary authorities prefer banknotes that are inexpensive to produce and other things equal, have a long life in circulation. These considerations make banknote design a mixture of art, science, politics and economics.[48] The life of banknotes according to study by P. Koeze depends on factors such as number of banknotes in circulation, wear and tear of the banknotes in the hands of the public, unfit banknotes withdrawn, unfit banknotes returned and total number of banknotes issued.
- **Demand for Banknote** - The demand for cash is made up of several components. Private consumption constitutes the primary one since cash is used to pay for various purchases and at least the demand for low-denomination banknotes appears to be primarily linked to retail payment transactions.[25] The Table 1 shows the growing demand for banknotes through production and supply data.

Table 1: Banknotes Produced and Supplied (in Billions of Pieces)

Year / Country	2000	2001	2002	2003	2004	2005	2006	2007	2008	2009
India	8.66	9.63	11.37	13.17	12.59	7.00	11.52	12.75	15.23	16.42

Source: Author's calculations on the basis of the Reserve Bank of India Annual Reports from 1999 to 2011.[40-42]

- **Banknote Production** - After World War II, it was the multi-colour intaglio process based on previous inventions by Orloff and Serge Beaune, promoted by Gualtiero Giori and cast in functioning machines by Koenig & Bauer that led to more standardized, wide-spread and modern banknotes, as we know them today.[37] As a result, a more pronounced specialization and differentiation of individual denominations have been observed recently in terms of security features and manufacturing cost.[37] Banknote printing requires a series of specialist printing processes including design, plate-making, printing process – offset printing, intaglio printing, letterpress printing, printed sheet examination and finished banknote sorting and packaging.[15,16]
- **Industry Structure** - Banknote printing has traditionally been carried out by governments or central banks. However, with the development of financial markets and the consolidation of specialized companies in banknote production, a number of central banks have invited private sector to participate in this function. Banknote printers can be classified into the following categories on the basis of their structural constitution.
    1. Owned by the government of the country of issue of banknote,
    2. Owned by the central bank, which issues the country's banknote,
    3. Owned by private enterprises and
    4. Jointly owned by central bank, government and private entrepreneurs.

1.2. Banknote Printing in India

Though India is using banknote in its modern form since 1861, banknote printing in India started in the year 1928 with the establishment of India Security Printing Press at Nashik. Until then the Indian currency notes were printed by Thomas De La Rue of United Kingdom. The following press report clearly states the conditions prevailing fifteen years ago and sets the tone for the present study. "Until 1996 the banknote printing and supply of India was not meeting the requirements of the Reserve Bank of India. The Currency Note Press, Nashik and Bank Note Press, Dewas could not fully meet the requirements of the central bank. Reserve Bank of India had to resort to get its supplies from sources abroad through international competitive bidding and awarded contracts in the year 1997. The Reserve Bank of India (RBI) has awarded the contract to print 3.6 billion currency notes worth Rs. 340 crore to nine foreign companies.[33]

Until 1996-97 it was the case of a single buyer and single government owned producer as seller. On recommendations of Expenditure Reforms Commission (ERC) appointed by the Government of India all the nine Security Units functioning under the administrative control of the Department of Economic Affairs, Ministry of Finance were taken over by the newly set up Corporation named as Security Printing and Minting Corporation of India – SPMCIL.[31] The Bharatiya Reserve Bank Note Mudran Private Limited-BRBNMPL came into being with two printing presses in the year 1996. This is a wholly owned subsidiary of Reserve Bank of India.

1.2.1. Security Printing and Minting Corporation of India (SPMCIL) - SPMCIL has an asset base of approximately Rs. 3000 crores and profit after tax of about Rs. 200 crores. The company is under the administrative control of Ministry of Finance, Department of Economic Affairs. SPMCIL is an industrial organization and is regulated in accordance with the prevalent labour laws. The Company has liabilities amounting to Rs. 3700 crores.[31] In the government system, annual budget for the corporation was to the tune of Rs. 1000 crores. The employee strength of SPMCIL is around 19000 in all nine units.[14] The annual licensed and installed capacity Currency Note Press is 4400 million pieces and production during 01.04.2007 to 31.09.2008 is 2929.375 million pieces. It has a history of printing currencies for other countries also.[47] The production of Bank Note Press was started in the year 1974 with annual licensed and installed capacity is 2495 million pieces of banknotes. This press also manufactures different types of security ink for various security organisations.[6]

1.2.2. Bharatiya Reserve Bank Note Mudran Private Limited (BRBNMPL) - Reserve Bank of India formed a wholly owned subsidiary company Bharatiya Reserve Bank Note Mudran Private Limited –BRBNMPL on 3rd February 1995. The present capacity of both the presses in 30 billion note pieces per year on a three shift basis.[9,10]

1.2.3. The Government - The Government of India manages seigniorage of the country and in this it is assisted by the Reserve Bank of India. Since July 2010 the currency and coinage issues are dealt by the Currency Directorate in the Department of Economic Affairs of Ministry of Finance. This directorate is responsible for issues of currency and coin, policy matters, production, planning and printing/minting of notes and coins. It has the administrative control of the Security Printing Minting Corporation of India Limited.[32]

1.2.4. Reserve Bank of India - Under the Reserve Bank of India Act (section 22), the Bank has the 'sole right' to issue currency notes in India.[45] Currency management has remained a major preoccupation of the central bank, a large proportion of whose staff was and continues to remain, deployed in this activity.[45] At present the Reserve Bank of India conducts bi-annual meetings with Ministry of Finance of Government of India where both SPMCIL and BRBNMPL present to decide the quantity of banknotes to be printed and supplied to RBI.[45]

1.2.5. Demand, Production and Supply of Banknotes in India - The banknote requirement and banknote printing industry are directly related to the economy of the country and are in tide with the economy. The quantity of banknotes in circulation in India since independence is given in Table 2.

1.2.6. Production Scenario - India is the second largest producer of banknotes in the world. Its annual production was 16,416 million pieces of banknotes in 2009-10, while the indent from the central bank was for 16,800 million pieces.

The Reserve Bank of India has incurred an expenditure of Rs. 27,540 million on printing banknotes. The quantity of banknotes printed and supplied by SPMCIL and BRBNMPL to the central bank has witnessed a steady growth during the period of study and their details of production and supply are given in Table 3. The annual demand of banknotes by Reserve Bank of India is given in the Table 4.

1.2.7. Security Features in Indian Banknotes - Reserve Bank of India introduced banknotes in the Mahatma Gandhi Series since 1996 in the denominations of Rs.5, Rs.10, Rs.20, Rs.50, Rs.100, Rs.500 and Rs.1000 which contain distinct and easily recognizable security features to facilitate the detection of genuine notes vis-à-vis forgeries. The 'new Mahatma Gandhi series' issued from 2005 in these seven denominations possesses security features which include Watermark, Security Thread, Latent Image, Microlettering, Intaglio, Identification Mark, Fluorescence, Optically Variable Ink and See through Register.[38]

Table 2: Banknote Circulation in India Compared with its GDP

Year	Banknotes in circulation	Growth in Circulation	GDP	Banknotes in circulation/ GDP
	Rupees in million	Percentage	Rupees in million	Percentage
1953-54	13300		110190	12.07
1955-56	16140	17.60	105180	15.35
1960-61	21540	25.07	165120	13.05
1965-66	28410	24.18	260470	10.91
1970-71	45570	37.66	429810	10.60
1975-76	70530	35.39	770710	9.15
1980-81	143070	50.70	1325200	10.80
1985-86	265240	46.06	2544270	10.42
1990-91	552820	52.02	5150320	10.73
1995-96	1225690	54.90	10832890	11.31
2000-01	2182050	43.83	19250170	11.34
2005-06	4295780	49.20	34023160	12.63
2009-10	7995490	46.27	58683320	13.62
Average for the 55 years		40.24		11.66

Source: Handbook of Statistics on the Indian Economy, Reserve Bank of India 2009-10 and author's calculations.

Table 3: Banknote Production and Cost in India

Year	Banknotes produced and supplied by SPMCIL and BRBNMPL	Change	Cost of banknotes produced	Change in
	Pieces in million	In Percentage	Rupees in million	Percentage
2000-01	8657		11210	
2001-02	9629	10.09	13340	15.97

2002-03	11370	15.31	14330	6.91
2003-04	13166	13.64	17100	16.20
2004-05	12593	-4.55	14440	-18.42
2005-06	7001	-79.87	10350	-39.52
2006-07	11522	39.24	20210	48.79
2007-08	12745	9.60	20320	0.54
2008-09	15225	16.29	20630	1.50
2009-10	16416	7.26	27540	25.09
Change between 2000-01 to 2009-10		89.63		145.67

Source: Annual Reports of Reserve Bank of India; Report of High level Committee to Reserve Bank of India, August 2009; Annual Reports of Security Printing and Minting Corporation of India; Annual Reports of Ministry of Finance, Government of India and author's calculations.

Table 4: Indent and Supply of Banknotes

Year	Demand by Reserve Bank of India	Change	Banknotes produced and supplied by SPMCIL and BRBNMPL	Demand of RBI met	Banknotes in Circulation	Change
	Pieces in million	In percentage	Pieces in million	In percentage	Pieces in million	In percentage
2000-01	*		8657		35704	
2001-02	10500		9629	91.70	38338	7.38
2002-03	13588	29.41	11370	83.68	37309	-2.68
2003-04	15800	16.28	13166	83.33	38336	2.75
2004-05	14855	-5.98	12593	84.77	36984	-3.53
2005-06	15000	0.98	7001	46.67	37851	2.34
2006-07	11500	-23.33	11522	100.19	39831	5.23
2007-08	12700	10.43	12745	100.35	44225	11.03
2008-09	15250	20.08	15225	99.84	48963	10.71
2009-10	16800	10.16	16416	97.71	56549	15.49
Average Change between 2000-01 to 2009-10		7.25		87.58		5.41

Source: Annual Reports of Reserve Bank of India; Report of High level Committee to Reserve Bank of India, August 2009; Annual Reports of Security Printing and Minting Corporation of India; Annual Reports of Ministry of Finance, Government of India and author's calculations. (*Data not found available)

1.2.8. Economics of Production and Supply of Banknotes - The banknote printing industry is controlled by a single source the Reserve Bank of India, who is the single buyer of this product. If there is only one customer for a certain good, that customer has a monopsony in the market for that good. A common theoretical implication is that the price of the good is pushed down near the cost of production. Market power is a continuum from perfectly competitive to monopsony. Reserve Bank of India exerts this power in abundance. The exercise of monopsony power results in prices being depressed below competitive levels.[35]

1.2.9. Measuring Monopsony Power - The usual index used to measure the extent of market power exercised by a seller is the Lerner Index. In the case of a monopolist, it can easily be shown that:

$$L = \frac{P-MC}{P} = \frac{1}{\eta}$$

where, the Lerner Index is the markup (price less marginal cost) as a percentage of price and it is equal to the inverse of the elasticity of demand (η). In the case of a monopsonist, the mirror image is the Buyer Power Index (BPI):

$$\lambda = \frac{VMP-w}{\lambda}$$

where, w is the factor price and VMP the value of marginal product. In a competitive market for a monopsonist it is easy to show that

$$VMP = w\lambda = 0$$

$$V = \frac{1}{\varepsilon}$$

where, ε is the elasticity of supply. Hence, as with a monopolist, the ability of a monopsonist to exercise buyer market power depends on the willingness and ability of the other side of the market to substitute. In the case of a monopsonist, the greater the inelasticity of supply, the less sensitive supply to price, the greater the exercise of monopsony power.[35]

2. LITERATURE REVIEW

It may not be an understatement to say that the printing industry is one of the least studied components of the manufacturing industry in India. A detailed discussion has been done based on the references as well as bibliography(*see* Annexure-I) ahead.

2.1. Money and Banknote

Money making as production operation has been dealt in detail by Klaus W. Bender in his Moneymakers: The Secret World of Banknote Printing (2006). It provides a critical snapshot of hitherto unexplored politico-economical and industrial business of banknote printing industry. The history of banknote production also has been dealt in detail in the Reserve Bank of India Volume I, Volume II and Volume 3 by S. L. N. Simha, G. Balachandran and RBI's History Cell.[2,39,45]

The websites of Security Printing and Minting Corporation of India Limited, Bharatiya Reserve Bank Note Mudran Private Limited, Currency Note Press, Nashik and Bank Note Press, Dewas have provided information on the banknote printing presses. Many occasional publications by European Central Bank, Bureau of Engraving and Printing, Reserve Bank of India occasional papers and Annual Reports of the Central banks of the world are also referred to, for studying different aspects of money, banknote production and currency management.

2.2. Banknote Production Methods

The developments in production methods of currency have been discussed in several publications of central banks. In fact, central banks and banknote printing presses rely on a variety of strategies to enhance efficiency in the production and supply of banknotes to the economy.[5]

These include, among others, creating subsidiary companies, turning production over to the private sector and combining currency printing and distribution under one roof, in a single complex. The central bank of Colombia examined these methods and strategies from a sample of 133 central banks between 1993 and 2003, finding out a tendency to turnover all or part of banknote production, primarily among central banks of developed countries in a broad study.[4]

At the Central Bank of Japan, Nishihara found that changes in the banknote printing methods in central banks of the Executives Meeting of East Asia and Pacific (EMEAP, composed of the central banks of Australia, China, Hong Kong S.A.R., Indonesia, Japan, South Korea, Malaysia, New Zealand, Philippines, Singapore and Thailand.) have developed on the central bank's relationship with the government, the financial sector and private companies, as well as the modernization strategy adopted by each central bank.[34]

2.3. Industry Economics

Banknote use propels answers to emerging newer efforts that search for adequate answers to emerging newer technological threats of counterfeiting.[43] These past and emerging threats provide the very structure for this industry of document security.

Jorge Eduardo Galán Camacho and Miguel Sarmiento Paipillauses, studied banknote printing costs and through comparative analysis showed that the major differences among central banks are primarily due to the size of the country's population and the amount of currency in circulation. The estimation of the cost function used, showed that the number of denominations and the size of banknotes are relevant factors in determining printing costs. They also showed that consequently, reductions in these characteristics lead to major cost savings.[36] Likewise, the method a central bank uses to produce banknotes also was found to be a determinant of printing costs. In fact, it was identified that government printing is the most costly method, while involving the private sector in the production process (e.g. joint ventures, subsidiaries, specialized companies) substantially reduces costs by the study.

The study by Jorge Eduardo Galán Camacho and Miguel Sarmiento Paipilla identifies possible strategies to reduce banknote printing costs and to perform this function more efficiently. Among the most important strategies are decreasing the number of denominations circulating in the economy, reducing the size of banknotes and involving the private sector to some extent in the production process.[36]

2.4. Industry Structure

Industry structure has been learnt from the Annual Reports of different central banks of the world and their publications including their annual reports have been extensively referred to in the present study. Also publications and press releases of RBI and Press Information Bureau have been referred to for notifications from the central bank and government respectively.

2.5. Denomination Structure

Annual Reports of different central banks have been referred to study the denomination structure of different banknote issuing countries and producers' industry statistics through industry publications are referred to and used in this paper.

2.6. Product Features

The security features and sizes of Indian banknotes have been sourced from RBI web sites, press releases and the web sites of the SPMCIL and BRBNMPL.

2.7. Production Function

"To the best of our knowledge, Nerlove [1963] is the first empirical study which uses cross section data of individual firms to investigate production technology. He estimates Cobb-Douglas cost function using 145 observations on American electric generating companies to analyze U.S. electric power industry, while Christensen and Greene (1976) and others extend it to employ the translog form".[28]

Aggregate production functions rely heavily on the use of marginal products and factor elasticities, both of which are microeconomic concepts that macroeconomists have found very useful for simplifying their models. While it is common practice to estimate these parameters for capital and labour in the whole economy, it is not entirely clear that these measurements capture an economically meaningful relationship. It is worth remembering that a production function does not express a relation between inputs and actual output, but between combinations of inputs and maximum potential output.[30]

The Cobb-Douglass function is still today the most ubiquitous form in theoretical and empirical analysis of growth and productivity. The estimation of the parameters of aggregate production functions is central too much of today's work on growth, technological change, productivity and labour. Empirical estimates of aggregate production functions are a tool of analysis essential in macroeconomics and important theoretical constructs, such as potential output, technical change or the demand for labour are based on them.[18]

Well-behaved production functions exist at the level of the firm. There are then two types of aggregation problems involved in the existence of an aggregate production function for the economy as a whole or even for some sector thereof. The first of these consists of aggregation over different factors to form aggregate labour or aggregate capital and of aggregation over different products to form aggregate output. This set of problems exists even at the level of the firm. The second problem consists of aggregation over firms. That is trivial if all factors and all outputs are continually re-assigned to firms to maximize efficiency, but this does not happen in practice (except, perhaps, when comparing situations of long run competitive equilibrium). In particular, different types of capital goods are associated with different techniques, and such capital goods are relatively fixed in place rather than constantly reallocated over firms.[20]

While, over some restricted range of the data, approximations may appear to fit, good approximations to the true underlying technical relations require close approximation to the stringent aggregation conditions and this is not a sensible thing to suppose. This is related to an old result of mine that, in simulation experiments, a Cobb-Douglas aggregate production function appears to work whenever factor shares are relatively constant, even though such an aggregate does not represent the underlying technological relationships at all well. Indeed, it explains the puzzle of some of those experiments that, while finding that same phenomenon, no similar organizing principle occurred when experimenting with CES functions.[19,21]

Given the structure of most growth models, we posit that the true relationship between capital and labour is likely to be close to Cobb-Douglas. Econometric estimation results lend support to the Cobb Douglas specification. Specifically, we fail to reject the Cobb-Douglas specification in 20 of the 28 industries and for seven of those industries we fail to reject the Leontief specification. We fail to reject Cobb-Douglas for aggregate manufacturing. Also, a comparison of econometric estimates and value-added weighted averages for several aggregations brings into question the common practice of averaging estimates for use in flexible aggregation models.[3]

Recently, Galán and Sarmiento, using a panel data model for 68 central banks during the period 2000-2004, found that the function of banknote printing is a very important determinant of the central bank's labour demand. Moreover, they found that a change in the strategy used to perform this function has a relevant effect on staff.[22] The case studies by Booth (1989)[7] and Lacker (1993)[29] for the United States are particularly important. Ericson (2004)[17] analyzed the banknote printing and currency management strategy adopted recently by the central bank of Sweden.

2.8. Printing Costs

Cost of printing of Indian banknotes has been obtained from the Annual Reports of the Reserve Bank of India; Annual Reports of the Department of Economic Affairs, Ministry of Finance in Government of India; Annual reports of the Security Printing and Minting Corporation of India since its formation and Handbook of Statistics on the Indian Economy by Reserve Bank of India.

2.9. Currency in Circulation, Population, GDP and Per capita GNP

Annual Reports of the Reserve Bank of India, its occasional papers, high level committee reports, Handbook of Statistics on the Indian Economy by Reserve Bank of India have been accessed for data on currency in circulation, population, GDP and per capita GNP for the purpose of the present study.

3. RESEARCH METHODOLOGY

The industry taken up for this study has a clear definition and standing in the field of industrial production and manufacturing. Its product is clearly unique and all the manufacturers available in this field of industry make an identical product and sell them to a same buyer. Also studying a manufacturing activity towards production function to ascertain cost is historic as has numerous examples from the past.

Present study also relies upon those earlier studies in identifying data for collection. The data available is basically from the sole and only buyer - the central bank, the government and the recently corporatized government corporation. According to the presenter of the study, the period from 2000 to 2010 is eventful if not path breaking. Also the data available are in Indian financial year basis.

3.1. Secondary Data

A wide range of journals on banknote printing industry, printing industry, newspapers, trade directories and studies, journals on economics of repute from both India and abroad, government publications, central bank publications from India and abroad, business magazines and secured web sites served as sources of secondary information. The previous ten years issues of the corporate journals, Reserve Bank of India's Annual Reports, Occasional Papers, Statistical Handbook on the Economy of India, Press Releases, Three Volume History of Reserve Bank of India and its web site were accessed for their wealth of data and information. Also the Annual Reports of the Ministry of Finance and its Annual Economic Surveys provided relevant data.

The Economic Census, Annual Survey of Industries, Index of Industrial Production and National Industrial Classification 2008 by the Central Statistical Organisation of Ministry of Statistics and Programme Implementation of Government of India were also referred. Publications of the All India Master Printers Association, British Printing Industries Federation, Graphic Arts Technical foundation of United States of America, PIRA International of United Kingdom and other world's leading printing industry bodies and establishments have also been studied.

3.2. Analytical Tools and Techniques and Employed

3.2.1. Cost Function for Banknote Printing

In order to suggest strategies to reduce printing costs and to enhance efficiency in the performance of this function, it is necessary to identify the variables that determine the printing costs. For this purpose, a cost function is estimated with a panel data model with random effects for banknote printing industry as whole in India, Security Printing and Minting Corporation of India and Bharatiya Reserve Bank Note Mudran Private Limited for the years from 2000-01 to 2009-10.

3.2.1.1. Banknote Printing as Manufacturing Activity - The process of inputting banknote paper and getting it impressioned with ink is an integrated system of economic activity whereby inputs are transformed into output of final goods and services ready for consumption is an economic activity governed by the usual computation of production, costs and returns.

Economic thinkers have, for the purpose of analysis, considered printing under a typical manufacturing activity in developing and developed countries. Shirkov (1973)[44] speaks about Indian Printing Industry under the category of manufacturing industry. Channon (1973)[12] discusses the structure of printing industries in Britain and America under the category of manufacturing industry. Boswell (1973)[8] also discusses the printing industry under the classification of manufacturing industry, in his analysis in a separate study.

3.2.1.2. Production Function in Banknote Printing - Production here includes total output of banknotes produced in a particular year including annual sale price of the banknotes. In this study the output is considered as the quantity of banknotes supplied by both the organizations to Reserve Bank of India.

Annual sale price is the amount for which the banknote denominations are sold to the Reserve Bank of India by both the producers and has been uniformly included for the purpose of analysis into total output. In computing production function, banknotes supplied to the Reserve Bank of India are considered.

The term output includes all expenses including wages plus manufacturing activity in the present analysis. As far as the knowledge of the author goes, so far only one study has been done on production function in printing titled 'An Economic Study of Printing Industry in Ramanathapuram District' as PhD dissertation by Joseph Soundara Rajan in the year 1984. This study deals exclusively with the printing industry of a particular district in southern part of India in Tamilnadu.[46]

3.2.1.3. Description of Production Function - A production function is an analytical tool which describes the maximum output that can be obtained from a given set of inputs in the existing state of technical knowledge.[26]

Output of an industry depends on fixed assets such as land, capital and other factors like organization and technological progress. The production function is a technical or engineering relation between input and output.[27] Mathematically; such a basic relationship between the inputs and output may be expressed as

$$Q = f(L, K, N, \ldots\ldots)$$

where, Q is Output; L is Labour; K is Capital; N is Land and other natural resources.

Hence, the level of output (Q), depends on the quantities of different inputs (L, K, N,........) available to the firm.

There are five different forms of production functions in the existing literature. Each depends on the substitutability of factors. They are: Linear Form of Production Function (Perfect Elasticity of Substitution), Leontif (Fixed coefficient) production function, Cobb-Douglas Production Function, Constant Elasticity of Substitution Production Function and Variable Elasticity of Production Functions.

The Cobb-Douglas Production Function is the commonly used function in the field of industrial economics. It is able to capture the flavour of essential non-linearities of the production process and yet benefits from the simplification of calculation from linear relationships by transforming to logarithms. The logarithmic function is linear in the parameters which is an essential point to economists. It has other merits like easy computational feasibility and possession of sufficient degree of freedom to allow for statistical testing. The Cobb-Douglas Function is convenient in inter-industry comparisons.[1]

Keeping these points in mind, Cobb-Douglas Function has been used in the present study. The cost of banknotes produced by the banknote printing industry in India depends on the following factors:
- Population of the country (*N*),
- Currency in circulation (*Circ*),
- Per capita income (*Y*),
- Number of denominations produced and circulating in the economy (*Den*),
- Average number of security features (*Sec*),
- Average size of the banknotes (*Size*) and
- The method used by the central bank to produce banknotes (*Sub* and *Gov*).

Other factors determining the production cost of the banknotes in India are wages of paid and distribution costs. These are appropriated in the form of production factors as listed above. Also the available data for the banknote costs are in the form of sale price paid by the Reserve Bank of India for the purchase of banknotes from SPMCIL and BRBNMPL. Accurate data for the wages and distribution are not available. Also the efficiency measures are not estimated and unavailable data about input prices, the variable (w) is omitted.

3.2.1.4. *The Model - Appropriation of Cobb Douglas Production Function*[18,30] - The printing cost function of banknote printing presses is assumed as a traditional Cobb-Douglas cost function, which is expressed as follows:

$$lnC(y,w) = \beta_0 + \beta_1 \cdot \ln(Y) + \sum_{i=1}^{n} \beta_i \cdot \ln(w_i)$$

---(1)

In the previous equation, *(Y)* represents the quantity of the final service or good produced and *(w)* the price is appropriated for this exercise *i* production factors. Cobb-Douglas cost function is used as it allows inferring directly about elasticities of the independent variables. For the econometric estimation, this function can be expressed as a log-linear equation, where a set of variables (Z) affecting production costs and out of the control of the bank, can be included.[13] Due to efficiency measures are not estimated and unavailable data about input prices, the variable (w) is omitted. Therefore, the following short term cost function is used:

$$\ln(C_{it}) = \beta_0 + \beta_1 \cdot \ln(Y_{it}) + \sum_{n=1j}^{m} \beta_j \cdot \ln(Z_{it}) + u_{it}$$

---(2)

Based on equation (2), variables that reflect the output level, the characteristics of the banknote production and the production methods used by the central banks are introduced in the model. The econometric model is:

$$Ln(C_{it}) = B_I + B_I\, Ln(N_{it}) + B_2\, Ln(Circ_{it}) + B_3\, Ln(Y_{it}) + B_4\, Ln(Sec_0) + B_5\, Ln(Size_0) + B_6. Sub_{it} + B_7. Gov_{it} + u_{it}$$

---(3)

In equation (3), the banknote costs (C) are function of: population of the country (*N*), currency in circulation (*Circ*), per capita income (*Y*), average number of security features (*Sec*), average size of the banknotes (*Size*) and the method used by the central bank to produce banknotes (*Sub* and *Gov*). The variable (*Sub*) refers to the method whereby subsidiary of Reserve Bank of India participate in the printing process. In this method the subsidiary is owned by the Reserve Bank of India and it purchases the outputs. This is a dummy variable that takes the value of 1 in either of the aforementioned cases and 0 in the other. Likewise, (*Gov*) is a dummy variable that specifically identifies the method in which the government is in charge of banknote printing; accordingly, it takes the value of 1 in that case and 0 in the other. The method whereby the central bank is in charge of printing all banknotes is the base case model. In other words, it is identified because, the (*Sub*) and (*Gov*) variables assume 0 value simultaneously.

The relation between the first two explicative variables (*N* and *Circ*) and costs was identified in the previous indicators. In the model these variables are introduced as *proxies* of the output level the central banks must supply to the economy and are expected to have a positive sign over them, in as much as the larger the country's population, the larger the quantity of banknotes required and therefore, the higher the costs. By the same token, if there is a large amount of currency circulating in the country's economy, the country's need for currency will be greater and consequently, so will production costs.

Gross National Per capita income (Y) is a variable used to identify the extent to which the financial development of an economy affects the printing costs. Usually, in more developed economies, the use of non-cash means of payment (e.g. electronic transfers and cards) is more prevalent; so, a negative sign is expected for this variable (*Note:* Evidence of this situation has been observed during recent years (*see* ECB, 2007, BIS 2007)). The number of denominations (*Den*) is also, to some extent, a measure of output, as the central bank has the obligation to supply banknotes of every existing denomination in circulation.

However, during the period considered for the present study and for a considerable period the number of denominations in circulation remained the same without change and therefore the introduction of this variable has not been taken up though considered for formulation of the function. A positive sign is expected due to, the more denominations, the higher the need for different types of plates, paper, ink combinations and time. The security features (*Sec*) and the size of banknotes (*Size*) are particular aspects of the product and are defined by the central bank. Lastly, the variables (*Sub* and *Gov*) are intended to find out if the methods used to produce banknotes determine their cost and which of those methods can represent greater benefits in terms of cost.

(C) is the dependent variable. (N), (Circ), (Y), (Sec), (Size) and (Sub and Gov) are independent variables. The function is estimated for the banknote printing industry in India as a whole taking data for a decade from 2000-01 to 2009-10 and for each of the two different production methods for government – SPMCIL and for the central bank owned subsidiary – BRBNMPL.

After taking logarithms, the above production function is estimated for by the principle of ordinary least squares. The values of B0, B1, B2, B3, B4, B5 and B6 are estimated for the banknote printing industry as whole and separately for SPMCIL and BRBNMPL. While estimating the values for each of the two methods of production, the proportionate values of population of the country and the currency in circulation are used.

3.2.1.5. Independent Variables

- **Printing Costs** - A comparative analysis of banknote printing costs is only provided for the Reserve Bank of India for the period from 2000-01 to 2009-10 with detailed information about their costs (*see* Table 5). Printing costs are those of producing banknotes directly or of being supplied with new banknotes, depending on the method used. When a central bank purchases banknotes from a private company, the amount it pays includes the company's profit margin.

When the government takes the responsibility for the production, the central bank usually recognizes only the production costs, or a part of them. When banknotes are produced by the central bank, the costs include production materials, depreciation of machinery and the cost of staff involved directly in production.

Firstly, costs are analyzed as an average for the period of study. Secondly, costs vary widely among banknote producers and the methods of production, as the quantities of banknotes produced are very different.

- **Population** - The country's population also is considered as measure of the quantity of banknotes required for the economy. Under this index, printing costs are compared to the population the Reserve Bank of India supplies banknotes.

Table 5: Banknote Printing Costs (Average 2000-01 to 2009-10)

Reserve Bank of India	Average printing costs per year in million Rupees[1]	Printing costs versus per capita GNP[2]	Cost per banknote produced in Rupees[3]
India	17440.00	0.055	1.21
SPMCIL	9699.33	0.031	1.46
BRBNMPL	7740.67	0.025	1.06

[1] Annual average cost in rupees.
[2] Cost per each banknote against average per capita GNP of the period.
[3] Average cost per each banknote produced, averaged over the period of study.
Source: Reserve Bank of India Annual Reports from 2000-01 to 2009-10); Ministry of Finance Annual Reports from 2000-01 to 2009-10; SPMCIL Annual Reports 2006-07 to 2009-10 and Author's calculations.

- **Currency in Circulation** - The level of currency in circulation is a good measurement of the quantity of banknotes a central bank must produce to satisfy the economy's currency needs. In fact, more currency in circulation implies more production and consequently, higher costs.
- **Per Capita Income** - This is the variable which is used as an indicator of level of economic development which will affect the cost of printing banknotes. An underdeveloped economies resort to cash transactions. Also this will have a bearing on the denomination structure and volume of different denominations to be printed. In these economies the life of banknotes, especially those of lower denominations will be lesser due to more soiling and wear and the demand for the lower denominations increases due to this reason also. A fast growing economy like India the economic growth coupled with inflation, results in the requirement of higher denomination banknotes. Therefore per capita income is a factor to be considered in deciding the cost of banknote production.

- **Number of Denominations Produced and Circulation in Economy** - Central banks must define the structure of denominations in circulation, regardless of the printing method used. Therefore, when drafting a production plan, it is essential to analyse the production needs for each denomination which are based on change in the quantity of banknotes demanded by the public; restocking deteriorated banknotes and the inventory needed to cover unexpected events which differs from one denomination to another. The number of denominations produced by the banknote presses remained constant at seven during the period of study.
- **Average Number of Security Features** - Central banks include security features on banknotes to prevent counterfeiting. Some are implicit in the paper manufacturing process (e.g. thickness, texture, inlays etc.); others, such as special inks, symbols, images, serial numbers and the like, are developed during the printing process and they determine some security features and the circulation life. (*see* Table 6)

Table 6: Security Features Most Commonly Used on Indian Banknotes

Features	
Watermark	Yes
Security threads	Yes
Intaglio printing	Yes
Micro inscription	Yes
Hidden image	Yes
Perfectly matched drawing	Yes
Identity mark	Yes
Optically variable ink	Yes
Fluorescence	Yes
Dual coloured optical fibre	Yes
Colour changing ink	Yes
Observation under ultraviolet light	Yes
Hologram (contrasting elements)	No
Average number of features	12

(Security features may vary among denominations.)
Source: Reserve Bank of India's Annual Reports (2000-2010) and its Press Releases and Occasional Publications (2000-2010).

- **Average Size of Banknote** - The size of banknotes is an aspect of the production process that banknote printers can control to reduce production resources (e.g. paper and ink). In many cases, the size of banknotes varies from one denomination to another. Nevertheless, cost considerations also influence the size of banknotes. Indian banknotes have remained the same in their size and therefore in their areas over a long period of time. Its banknote sizes match those of the developed countries and its average banknotes size remains at 103.67 square centimetres like those of Euro banknotes of 105.58 square centimetres.

- **The Method used by the Presses to produce Banknotes** - The printing press which produces the banknotes can be owned and managed by the government, the central bank or a private producer. India had until recently used government printing presses and foreign private printers as has been detailed in the previous chapters. Currently the methods of production used for printing banknotes in India are 1.
Government owned Security Printing and Minting Corporation of India – SPMCIL and 2. Reserve Bank of India owned Bharatiya Reserve Bank Note Mudran Private Limited - BRBNMPL. While the SPMCIL has other products in addition to banknotes BRBNMPL survives solely on printing banknotes.

3.3. Statistical Methods

The data collected were coded, tabulated and analysed using statistical techniques as detailed in above sections. The statistical tools employed included multiple regression analysis,[23] and t-tests.[24] The data were recorded and transformed to suit the use of such statistical techniques.

Multiple regression analysis tests were carried out using Smith's Statistical Package, Version 2.80, September 26, 2005 by Gary Smith and other computer applications wherever needed. The method underlying the analysis of the data has been introduced in the preceding sections.

3.4. Implications of the Analysis

The above computations provided the basis for subsequent analysis and were found to be useful in answering the following:

"What is the production cost function for the banknote printing industry in India and its constituents and their weightage in influencing the cost of production?"

3.5. Limitations of the Study

The present study has not covered all the aspects of the banknote printing industry in India which is other than production cost function. Therefore this is not an all-encompassing study. Also this has not dealt into the industrial aspects of technology, manpower, skill factors, knowhow, machineries and other capital equipments and their performance.

4. RESULTS, ANALYSIS AND DISCUSSION

The data were interpolated to the framework as required and the results were obtained. Each of the hypotheses has been considered using these methodologies in arriving at the results.

4.1. Results of Cost Function Analysis

The proposed econometric model is:

$Ln(C_{it}) = B_0 + B_1.Ln(N_{it}) + B_2.Ln(Circ_{it}) + B_3.Ln(Y_{it}) + B_4.Ln(Sec_{it}) + B_5Ln(Size_{it}) + B_6.Sub_{iv\ it}$

(4)

---(4)

For the above cost function values of B0, B1, B2, B3, B5, B6 and B8 are estimated for the banknote printing industry as whole and separately for SPMCIL and BRBNMPL. Equation (4) above was estimated through the generalized least squares method (GLS). The results in Table 7 show a well modelled specification and a high joint significance of variables. The population and circulation coefficients were positive and significant with a 99% confidence level. This indicates they are good approximations to output and have a positive impact on costs.

Table 7: Estimated Values of the Coefficients of Cost Function for Banknote Printing Industry in India

	Indian Banknote Printing Industry				
	Dependent variable: Ln(C)				
	Observations: 10, Multiple Regression Equation				
	Industry	t value	Std. error	One-sided p value	R- squared
Intercept	130375.9417	0.7956	163865.2599	0.2354	
Ln (N)	-23.0228	0.1585	145.2586	0.4409	0.9775
Ln (Circ)	0.0000	0.6747	0.0000	0.2684	0.9377
Ln (Y)	0.1177	1.1876	0.0991	0.1503	0.9896
Ln (Sec)	-4002.4319	1.4081	2842.4767	0.1159	0.8669
Ln (Size)	-486.0205	0.8254	588.8531	0.2278	0.4815
Standard error of estimate					3279.6700
Coefficient of determination R- squared					0.8830
Adjusted determination coefficient of $\bar{R}$–squared (Adjusted degrees of freedom)					0.73675

Source: Author's Calculations on the Basis of Data Collected

The population and the security features incorporated and the size have negative coefficients. This suggests that the increase in population will result in reduction in production cost as is the case regarding the banknote size and number of security features. While the increase in income will have a positive effect on cost, the currency in circulation has no effect on the cost of printing. Contrary to expectations, the coefficient of the variable including the number of security features is negative and not significant. So, the variable is not a relevant determinant of costs.

However, it is possible that what determines printing costs is the kind of security features used instead of the number. Unfortunately, this detailed information is hard to introduce in the model. Banknote size, is a variable pretending to detect an important feature of the product was also proved to be not significant and not with the expected sign. In other words the central bank's decision about the size of banknotes does not have a major impact on printing costs. This may be due to the huge population which can absorb even more banknotes than existing thereby achieving economies of scale. However, adopting a smaller size of banknotes is a valid strategy to reduce those costs.

One of the model's most relevant results concerns the intercept is that it is positive and it affects the costs as a positive constant and the standard error of estimate is found to be 3279.6700. The Reserve Bank of India procures banknotes from both its subsidiary and the government company paying different prices. The coefficient is worked out on the basis of the total banknote printed and supplied and the overall price the RBI had paid to both the producers. Therefore the coefficients for both the printers have been worked out separately in the following paragraphs.

4.1.1. *Security Printing and Minting Corporation of India*

The population and the size have negative coefficients. This suggests that the increase in population will result in reduction in production cost as is the case regarding the banknote size. While the increase in income will have a positive effect on cost, the currency in circulation has no effect on the cost of printing. Unlike the industry as whole the number of security features has a positive coefficient thereby influencing the costs positively. More the number of security features introduced the price of the banknote tends to go up. In this case also contrary to expectations, the coefficient of the variables population and banknote size are negative and not significant. So, the variable is not a relevant determinant of costs for printing of banknotes at SPMCIL. However, it has become clear that what determines printing costs is the kind and number of security features.

Banknote size, is a variable pretending to detect an important feature of the product was also proved to be not significant and not with the expected sign. However the significance value of – 463.3966 of SPMCIL is higher than that of the industry value which is -4002.4319. Therefore the central bank's decision about the size of banknotes does have a lesser impact on printing costs. This may be due to the huge population which can absorb even more banknotes than existing thereby achieving economies of scale.

One of the model's most relevant results concerns the intercept is that it is positive at 49880.854 which is lesser than the industry and it affects the costs as a positive constant and the standard error of estimate is found to be 1656.0493 which is also lesser than the industry value of 3279.6700, thereby ensuring a better fit of this model. The price of the banknotes paid by the Reserve Bank of India this government company is higher than that of the industry average and that of the subsidiary company. (*see* Table 8)

Table 8: Estimated Values of the Coefficients of Cost Function for Security Printing and Minting Corporation of India

	Security Printing and Minting Corporation of India				
	Dependent variable: Ln(C)				
	Observations: 10, Multiple Regression Equation				
	Industry	Std. error	t value	One-sided p value	R- squared
Intercept	49880.854	31105.2595	1.6036	0.0920	
Ln (N)	-2.3726	26.6085	0.0892	0.4666	0.9595
Ln (Circ)	-0.0000	0.0000	0.2469	0.4086	0.9893
Ln (Y)	0.0305	0.0488	0.6254	0.2828	0.9890
Ln (Sec)	57.3710	1748.4808	0.0328	0.4877	0.9103
Ln (Size)	-463.3966	304.1851	1.5234	0.1012	0.5046
Standard error of estimate					1656.0493
Coefficient of determination R- squared					0.8438
Adjusted determination coefficient of $\bar{R}$–squared (Adjusted degrees of freedom)					0.64855

Source: Author's Calculations on the Basis of Data Collected

4.1.2. *Bharatiya Reserve Bank Note Mudran Private Limited*

The population and the security features incorporated and the size have negative coefficients (*see* Table 9). This suggests that the increase in population will result in reduction in production cost as is the case regarding the banknote size and number of security features. While the increase in income will have a positive effect on cost, the currency in circulation has no effect on the cost of printing. In this case too, contrary to expectations, the coefficient of the variable including the number of security features is negative and not significant. So, the variable is not a relevant determinant of costs. However, it is possible that what determines printing costs is the kind of security features used instead of the number.

Table 9: Estimated Values of the Coefficients of Cost Function for Bharatiya Reserve Bank Note Mudran Private Limited

	Bharatiya Reserve Bank Note Mudran Private Limited Dependent variable: Ln(C) Observations: 10, Multiple Regression Equation				
	Industry	Std. error	t value	One-sided p value	R- squared
Intercept	-18638.2594	28342.2629	0.6576	0.2734	
Ln (N)	-24.2471	21.5651	1.1244	0.1619	0.8725
Ln (Circ)	-0.0000	0.0000	0.7227	0.2549	0.9845
Ln (Y)	0.0803	0.0322	2.4928	0.0336	0.9833
Ln (Sec)	-1803.5570	823.6731	2.1897	0.0469	0.7316
Ln (Size)	423.4300	359.8318	1.1767	0.1523	0.7649
Standard error of estimate					1349.4804
Coefficient of determination R- squared					0.9410
Adjusted determination coefficient of $\bar{R}$–squared (Adjusted degrees of freedom)					0.86725

Source: Author's Calculations on the Basis of Data Collected

Banknote size is a variable pretending to detect an important feature of the product was proved to be significant and is with the expected sign. In other words the central bank's decision about the size of banknotes does have a major impact on printing costs. This may be due to efficiency of BRBNMPL and its capacity to vary the production cost of the product by efficient means of performance. Therefore, adopting a smaller size of banknotes is a valid strategy to reduce those costs. The model's most relevant results concerns the intercept is that it is negative and it affects the costs as a negative constant and the standard error of estimate is found to be 1349.4804 which is the least of all the three instances, meaning more reliability on the model. The subsidiary firm of Reserve Bank of India seems to efficient than its co-producer SPMCIL and is more efficient than the industry and it can produce banknotes at lesser prices than the government company and the industry average.

4.2. Cost Function

It was identified that India has just sufficient capacity to cater to its banknote printing requirements which are growing rapidly. With the growth in demand which is less than the growth of GDP the cost of the banknote printing mainly depends on its per capita income, size of the banknotes and to a certain extent on the number of security features. Banknote printing presses functioning as subsidiaries of the central bank are more efficient and at less cost while that of the government owned companies are less in efficiency and their products cost more. Also the government companies in this industry are price setters while the subsidiary presses are price getters. There are important but different effects of security features on banknote printing presses which vary depending on the nature of ownership of the firm. This is also true with regard to size of the banknotes. Per capita income has a positive bearing on the cost of the banknote production cost.

On the other hand, the comparative analysis of the banknote printing costs did not show major differences among the industry as whole and the other two firms namely SPMCIL and BRBNMPL primarily due to the size of the population and the amount of currency in circulation. The estimation of the cost functions showed that the sizes of banknotes and number security features are relevant factors determining the cost of printing. Consequently, reductions in these characteristics shall lead to major cost savings. Likewise, the nature of ownership of firms printing the banknotes for central bank was found to be determinant of printing costs. In fact, it was identified that government printing is the costlier method and the subsidiary company involved in the printing of banknotes substantially reduces costs.

The population though has negative significance in all the three analyses it has the most negative effect in the case of BRBNMPL thereby signifying its productive efficiency. It also may be the case that of increasing returns to scale and efficiency. Per capita income in general has a positive significance on all the three occasions thereby it can be clearly concluded that per capita income has a positive effect on the price of the banknote. But the increase varies the most in case of industry and the least in case of SPMCIL. The number of banknotes in circulation has no significance on the price of the banknote according to this model returning with significance levels of 0.00 on all three instances.

On the other hand the number of security features turned out to be most significant in case of SPMCIL and with negative significance for industry as a whole and for BRBNMPL. The significance of the size of the banknote is negative for the industry and for SPMCIL almost at similar levels signifying inefficient and high cost performance of the government company. It has a positive significance with regard to BRBNMPL.

The reduction in size of the banknote printed by BRBNMPL will have a reduction in price and for increase in size the price too will increase. This again signifies the performance efficiency of the subsidiary of a monopsony buyer to supply banknotes at lower costs when the size is reduced. Also this implies that the inefficiency of the government company which cannot vary its price even if the sizes are altered.

Overall it is learnt that the currency in circulation has no impact on the price. But it may be influenced by the nature of the security feature incorporated in the banknote which has not been included in the scope. Unfortunately, this detailed information is hard to introduce in the model.

5. CONCLUSION

India has one of the finely managed currencies in the world. With both the supply and demand sides performing in tandem India can be considered a banknote printing superpower. It has mastered the use of controlling all the required variables used in the banknote production including namely, population, banknote in circulation, increasing per capita income, steady number of denominations and experience of producing banknotes in government owned and central bank subsidiary printing presses. But it faces the challenge and threat of fast outdating of technologies of printing of banknotes and threat of counterfeiting due to the latest 'off the shelf' printing technologies. This is coupled with the growing over capacity of banknote printing in the world and the single (monopsony) buyer demanding cheaper banknotes at world class qualities is a concern for the Indian banknote printing presses. Still the dependence on machinery and equipment from foreign suppliers is to be overcome which may take a considerable time.

Therefore, the presenter feels the need for increasing the effort on research and developments in all aspects of banknote printing to focus on development of new cost efficient and better performing security features, long lasting substrates, optimising banknote sizes, development of state of the art quality assurance and quality control systems and production of raw materials which are cost effective and secured in the short and medium terms. In doing so it has to consider the developments which are taking place in other areas of the central banking, finance and general monetary developments in India and abroad.

5.1. Scope for Further Research

The present study has covered only one aspect of the banknote printing industry in India which is production cost function. Therefore this is not an all-encompassing study. The areas of technology used and their performance in relation to the availability of the technology in India needs to be looked into for a deeper study. The industry's supply chain and storage and distribution is an important area of its functioning need an elaborate study. The effect of counterfeits on the banknote producer and response by the banknote producer and the central bank is an interesting area of study. The optimal structure for the banknote printing industry and the optimal product mix for the industry and for its firms requires a study in depth.

5.2. Acknowledgements

The author profusely acknowledges his mentor Dr. C. K. Renukarya, Professor of Economics and Director, Pooja Bhagavat Memorial Mahajana Post Graduate Centre, K. R. S. Road, Mysore – 570016 for the invaluable and immeasurable support, guidance and advices received from him and Dr. Anjila Gupta, Professor of Economics & Discipline Coordinator, School of Social Sciences, IGNOU, Maidan Garhi, New Delhi – 110068 for her unstinting support and guidance. It may not be not of place to acknowledge and state the invaluable words of inspiration and support received from Dr. Kaustava Barik, Department of Economics, School of Social Sciences, IGNOU, Maidan Garhi, New Delhi – 110068 in doing this paper. Last but not the least I would heartily acknowledge the great inspirations I have been receiving from Dr. Gopinath Pradhan, Director, School of Social Sciences, IGNOU, Maidan Garhi, New Delhi – 110068 since my enrolment as a doctoral scholar. My source of lifelong affection, fountainhead of inspiration and support from family members is worth mentioning.

6. REFERENCES

1. Agrawal HS. (1978). "*A Mathematical Approach to Economic Theory*", First edition ed., Lakshmi Narain Agarwal Educational Publishers, Agra.
2. Balachandran G. (1998). "*The Reserve Bank of India 1951-1967*", Oxford University Press, Delhi.
3. Balistreri EJ, McDaniel CA, and Wong EV. (2002). "An Estimation of US Industry- Level Capital Labor Substitution Elasticities: Cobb-Douglas as a Reasonable Starting Point?", Working Paper, Accessed through: http://ideas.repec.org/p/wpa/wuwpco/0303001.html
4. Banco de la República. (2005). "*Tendencias en Funciones y Planta de Personal de Bancos Centrales*", Banco de la República, Department of Planning and Budget, Banco de la República, Bogotá, D.C..
5. Baxter AG. (2005). "Alternative Models for Outsourcing Banknote Services' in Central Bank Modernisation", Courtis NA, ed., Central Banking Publications, London.
6. BNP Dewas. (n.d.). "*About Us*". Accessed on February 12 2010, through bnpdewas.spmcil.com: http://bnpdewas.spmcil.com/SPMCIL/interface/AboutUs.aspx
7. Booth G. (1989). "*Currency and Coin Responsibilities of the Federal Reserve: A historical Perspective*", Federal Reserve Bank of Cleaveland, Cleaveland.
8. Boswel J. (1973). "*The Rise and Decline of Small Firms*", George Allen and Unwin Ltd., London.
9. BRBNMPL. (2011). "*Welcome to BRBNMPL*", accessed on February 15 2013, through https://www.brbnmpl.co.in/default.aspx
10. BRBNMPL. (n.d.). "*History*", accessed on July 21 2011, through https://www.brbnmpl.co.in/asp/viewContent.asp?pageId=3&headId=3
11. Central Statistical Organisation. (2008). "*National Industrial Classification (All Economic Activities) 2008*", September, Ministry of Statistics and Programme Implementation, Government of India, New Delhi.
12. Channon DF. (1973). "*The Strategy and Structure of British Enterprise*". Macmillan Press India Limited, London.
13. Coelli TB. (1995). "A Model for Technical Inefficiency Effects in a Stochastic Frontier Production Function for Panel Data", *Empirical Economics*, Vol.20, pp.325-332.
14. Currency Note Press. (n.d.). "History", accessed on February 12 2010, through cnpnashk.spmcil.com: http://cnpnashk.spmcil.com/SPMCIL/interface/History.aspx
15. De La Rue plc. (2010). "*Annual Report 2010*", De La Rue plc, Basingstoke.
16. De La Rue Plc. (n.d.). "*The Banknote Lifecycle*", accessed on August 29 2011, through http://www.delarue.com/ProductsSolutions/BanknoteProduction/TheBanknoteLifecyc/
17. Ericson SD. (2004). "Cash-supply Efficiency", *Economic Review*, Vol.(3), pp.27-42.
18. Felipe J, and Adams FG. (2005). "The Estimation of the Cobb-Douglas Function: A Retrospective View", *Eastern Economic Journal*, Vol.31(3), pp.427-445.
19. Fisher FM. (1971). "Aggregate Production Functions and the Explanation of Wages: A Simulation Experiment", *Review of Economics and Statistics*, Reprinted in Fisher [1992-93], pp.305-325.
20. Fisher FM. (2005). "Aggregate Production Functions - A Pervasive, but Unpesurvasive Fairytale", *Eastern Economic Journal*, Vol.31(3), p.489.
21. Fisher FM, Solow RM, and Kearl JR. (1978). "Aggregate Production Functions: Some CES Experiments", *Review of Economic Studies*, June, Reprinted in Fisher [1992-93], pp.305-320.

22. Galán JA. (2007). "Staff, Functions, and Staff Costs at Central Banks: An International Comparison with a Labor-demand Model", *Money Affairs*, Vol.XX(2), pp.131-180.
23. http://department.obg.cuhk.edu.hk/researchsupport/Paired_t_test.asp, accessed on September 12 2011.
24. http://www.xuru.org/rt/MLR.asp, accessed on September 12 2011.
25. Jefferson PN. (2004). "Attachment to a National Money: Evidence on Currency Holding at Different Levels of Development", *Review of Development Economics*, Vol.8(2), pp.179-197.
26. Katz JM. (1969). *"Production Functions, Foreign Investment and Growth"*, North-Holland Publishing Company, Amsterdam.
27. Klein LR. (1962). *"An introduction to Econometrics"*, Prentice Hall.
28. Konishia Y, and Nishiyama Y. (2002). "Nonparametric Test for Translog specification of Production Function in Japanese Manufacturing Industry", *Op cite*, pp.597-602.
29. Lacker J. (1993). "Should we Subsidize the Use of Currency?", *Economic Quarterly*, Vol.Winter, pp.47-73.
30. Miller E. (2008). *"An Assessment of CES and Cobb-Douglas Production Functions"*, Congressional Budget Office.
31. Ministry of Finance. (2006). *"Annual Report 2005-06"*, March, Ministry of Finance, Government of India, New Delhi.
32. Ministry of Finance. (2011). *"Annual report 2010-11"*, August 29, Ministry of Finance, Government of India, New Delhi.
33. Mohan AN. (1997)." Thomas De La Rue, 8 others bag currency printing bid", May 8, Indian Express.
34. Nishihara R. (2006). *"Central Bank Services-Focusing on Core Banking Operations: Cash"*, May, Bank of Japan.
35. Organisation for Economic Co-operation and Development. (2009). *"Monopsony and Buyer Power"*, December 17, Directorate for Financial and Enterprise Affairs, Competition Committee.
36. Paipilla JE. (2007). *"Banknote Printing at Modern Central Banking: Trends, Costs and Efficiency"*, September 10-14, *Borradores de Economia*, Vol.476.
37. Pohl W. (2009). *"Trends and Tendencies in Banknote Production"*, July 30, Security Printing KG, assessed through www.sp-kg.de
38. Raghuraj G. (2006). *"Press Release: 2005-2006/189"*, Deputy General Manager, Reserve Bank of India, accessed through http://rbidocs.rbi.org.in/rdocs/Pressrelease/PDFs/65203.pdf.
39. Rangarajan DC. (2005). *"The Reserve Bank of India 1967-1981"*, Vol.(3), The Reserve Bank of India, Mumbai, Maharashtra.
40. Reserve Bank of India. (1999-2000 to 2011-2012). *"Annual Reports"*, Reserve Bank of India, Mumbai.
41. Reserve bank of India. (2010). *"Annual Report 2009-10"*, Reserve Bank of India, Mumbai.
42. Reserve Bank of India. (2011). *"RBI Monetary Museum, Contemporary Currency, Frequently Asked Questions"*, accessed on July 25 2011, through: http://www.rbi.org.in/scripts/PrintView.html
43. Schell KJ. (2007). *"History of Document Security"*, in Leeuw KD, and Karl de Leeuw JA. (Ed.). *"The History of Information Security: A Comprehensive Handbook"*, Elsevier, pp.198-214.
44. Shirkov GK. (1973). *"Industrialisation of India"*, Progress Publishers, Moscow.
45. Simha SL. (1970). "History of The Reserve Bank of India, 1935-1951", Vol.1, Reserve Bank of India, Bombay, India.

46. SoundaraRajan LJ. (1984). "An Economic Study of Printing Industry in Ramanathapuram District", February, *PhD. Dissertation*, Madurai Kamaraj University.
47. SPMCIL. (2008). "Annual Report 2007-08", Security Printing and Minting Corporation of India.
48. Williams MM, and Anderson RG. (2007). "Handicapping Currency Design: Counterfeit Deterrence and Visual Accessibility in the United States and Abroad", *Working Paper*, Federal Reserve Bank of St. Louis, Research Division, St. Louis, P.O. Box 442, MO 63166011B.

Annexure – I
BILIOGRAPHY

1. Aigner DL. (1977). "Formulation and Estimation of Stochastic Frontier Production Function Models", *Journal of Econometrics*, Vol.6, pp.21-37.
2. Anderson MM. (2007). *"Handicapping Currency Design: Counterfeit Deterrence and Visual Accessibility in the United States and Abroad"*, Research Division, March, P.O. Box 442, St.Louis, MO 63166011B: Federal Reserve Bank of St. Louis.
3. Arjowiggins Graphic. (2011). *"Innovation for our clients"*, Arjowiggins Graphic, June 6.
4. Asian Development Bank. (2003). *"Asian Development Outlook"*, Asian Development Bank, Manila.
5. Banco Centro Brazil. (2003). *"Polymer Banknote: Two Years of Brazilian Experience"*, Currency Management Department, February, Banknote 2003, Washington.
6. Bank of England. (2010). *"Take a Closer Look. Take a Closer Look - Your Easy-to- Follow Guide to Checking Banknotes"*, March, Bank of England, United Kingdom.
7. Bank of England. (2010). *"Annual Report 2010"*, June, Bank of England.
8. Bank of England. (2010). *"Annual Report 2009"*, May, Bank of England.
9. Bank of Thailand. (n.d.). *"Banknotes - Production and Security"*, accessed on August 29 2011, through http://www.bot.or.th/English/Banknotes/production_and_security/NPT_BankOfThailand/Pages/Banknote_production_process.aspx
10. Banker RC. (1984). "Some Models for Estimating Technical and Scale Inefficiencies in Data Envelopment Analysis", *Management Science*, Vol.9(30), pp.1078-1092.
11. Berger AA. (1997). "Inside the Black Box: What Explains Differnces in the Efficiencies of Financial Institutions?", *Journal of Banking and Finance*, Vol.(21), pp.895-947.
12. Bohn JH. (2001). "Estimates of Scale and Cost Efficiency for Federal Reserve Currency Operations", *Economic Review*, Vol.IV, pp.2-26.
13. Booysen F. (2002). "An Overview and Evaluation of Composite Indices of Development", *Social Indicators Research*, Vol.59, pp.115-151.
14. Bose U. (1976). *"Problems of Printing Industry in Uttar Pradesh with Special reference to Allahabad"*, accessed through http://www.vidyanidhi.org.in/.
15. Buckley PJ. Pass CL, and Prescott K. (1988). "Measures of International Competitiveness: A Critical Survey", *Journal of Marketing Management,* Vol.4(2), pp.175-200.
16. Bureau of Engraving and Printing. (2004). *"BEP History"*, Historical Resource Center, Bureau of Engraving and Printing.
17. Bureau of Engraving and Printing. (2011). *"2010 CFO Report"*, Department of Treasury, Bureau of Engraving and Printing, Washington D.C., USA, 20228.
18. Bureau of Engraving and Printing. (2005). *"Performance and Accountability Report"*, Chief Financial Officer, Department of Treasury.

19. Byars L. (1991). *"Strategic Management: Formulation and Implementation, Concepts and Cases"*, 3rd edition, HarperCollins Publisher Inc., New York.
20. Caltin C. (2007). *"Co Processing of Paper and Polymer Banknote. A Systems Approach"*, PolyTeQ Services, October, Global Technology Support for Guardian Polymer Substrate.
21. Carlin P. (2004). "Currency Note Processing and Distribution Arrangements in Australia", May, Note Issue Department, Reserve Bank of Australia.
22. Caves DC. (1982). "The Economic Theory of Index Numbers and the Measurement of Input, Output and Productivity", *Econometrica*, Vol.50(6), pp.1393-1414.
23. Chant J. (2004). *"Counterfeiting: A Canadian Perspective"*, September, Bank of Canada.
24. Charnes A, Cooper WW, and Rhodes E. (1978). "Measuring the Efficiency on Decision Making Units", *European Journal of Operational research*, Vol.2(4), pp.429-444.
25. China Banknote Printing and Minting Corporation. (2007). accessed on May 02, through http://syzb.cbpmc.com.cn/english.htm
26. Commission of the European Communities. (2007). "Five Years of Euro Banknotes and Coins", February 20, European Central Bank, Brussels.
27. Cooper WW, Seiford LM, and Tone K. (2000). *"Data Envelopment Analysis: A Comprehensive text with models, applications, references and DEA-solver software"*, Kluwer Academic Publishers.
28. Crane Currency. (n.d.). accessed on August 29 2011, through Paper Manufacturing: http://www.crane.se/pa.html
29. Cukrowski J. (1999). *"Central Bank Seigniorage: Czech Republic 1993-1997"*, March, JEL Classification: E58, F36, P51.
30. Dalmau Porta JI, Segarra Oña M, and De Miguel Molina B. (n.d.). "Analysis of the Competitiveness of the Home Furniture Industry in the Valencian Economy", *41st Congress of the European Regional Science Association*, Politechnical University of Valencia, Spain, p.17.
31. Department of Trade and Industry. (1994). "Competitiveness", HMSO, London, Cm 2563.
32. Department of Treasury. (2004, 2006, 2007, 2008, 2009 and 2010). *"Performance and Accountability Report"*, Chief Financial Officer, Bureau of Engraving and Printing.
33. Douglas PH. (1948). "Are There Laws of Production?", *American Economic Review*, Vol.38(1), pp.1-41.
34. Eckhard S. (2003). "Concepts and Measurements of Competitiveness and Comparative Advantage: Towards an Integrated Approach", *International Industrial Organization Conference*, Northeastern University, Massachusetts, Boston.
35. Economides N. (2001). "The Impact of the Internet on Financial Markets", *Journal of Financial Transformation*, Vol.1(1), pp.8-13.
36. Elizabeth A, and Coleman IG. (2008). "Report on the Control review of the Boards Currency Expenditures and Assessments", September.
37. European Central Bank. (1997), July 2, accessed on April 26 2007, through: https://www.ecb.int/press/pr/date/1997/html/pr970702_4.en.html
38. European Central Bank. (2005). "Recycling of Euro Banknotes: Framework for the Detection of Counterfeits and Fitness Sorting by Credit Institutions and Other Professional cash Handlers", January, European Central Bank, accessed through http://www.euro.ecb.int
39. European Central bank. (2007). "Our Money - Trainer's Guide to the Euro Banknotes and Coins. Retrieved 2010", July, European Central Bank, accessed through http://www.euro.ecb.int
40. Evans D. (2008). "A Short History of Barter as Money", August 11, Specialist Economic Advisors, accessed on 2009, through www.spec-adv.com, Page 5.
41. Expenditure and Reforms Commission. (2000). "Restructuring of the Department of Economic Affairs", December 22, Ministry of Finance, Government of India, New Delhi.
42. Fare RS. (1989). "Productivity Developments in Swedish Hospitals: A Malmquist Output Index Approach", *Discussion Paper No. 89-3*, Southern Illinois University, Illinois.

43. Freudenberg M. (2003). *"Composite Indicators of Country Performance: A Critical Assessment"*, Directorate for Science, Technology and Industry. Organization for Economic Cooperation and Development (OECD), Paris.
44. Gajjar T. (2004). "Art of Printing: Its Origin and Development in the Context of Advertising", Varanasi, accessed through: http://www.vidyanidhi.org.in/.
45. Gelei A. (2003). "Competitiveness: A Match between Value Drivers and Competencies In The Hungarian Automotive Supply Chain", Budapest University of Economic Sciences and Public Administration, Hungary.
46. Gieseke, and Devrient. (2011). "Annual Report 2010", Gieseke & Devrient Group, Munich, Germany.
47. Goznak. (2007). accessed on april 25, through: http://www.goznak.ru/main.php?page=288
48. Grant RM. (1996). "Toward a Knowledge Based Theory of Firm", *Strategic Management*, Vol.17, pp.109-122.
49. Gupta A. (2008). *"Looking Beyond the Methods: Productivity estimates and Growth Trends in Indian Manufacturing"*, October, University of British Columbia. Vancouver.
50. Heij HA. (2000). "The Design Methodology of Dutch Banknotes", January, *Proceedings of SPIE*, SPIE, San Jose, California, Vol.3973, pp.27-28.
51. Heij HA. (2005). "Life Cycle Analysis of Security Features in Banknotes - from Central Bank to Cashier", 20-23 February, *Banknote 2005*, De Nederlandsche Bank NV, Washignton D.C., USA.
52. Heij HA. (2007). "Public Feedback of Better Banknote Design", *DNB Occasional Studies*, Vol.5(2).
53. Heij HA. (2010). "Innovative Approaches to the Selection of Banknote Security Features", presented at *Banknote conference*.
54. Henderson R, and Cockburn LM. (2000). *"Disentangling the Origins of Competitive Advantage"*, *Strategic Management Journal*, Special Issue on The Evolution of Firm Capabilities, Vol.15, pp.143-152.
55. HKMA. (n.d.). *"Hong Kong Monetary Authority"*, accessed on September 08 2011, through 2010 Series Hong Kong Banknotes: http://www.info.gov.hk/hkma/eng/currency/2010_series/index.htm
56. Hologram Industries. (2011). *"Fiduciary Documents"*, September 13, accessed through Anti-Counterfeiting Solutions: http://www.hologram-industries.com/
57. Hueck Folien. (n.d.). *"Engineered films, Material with IQ"*, accessed on September 13 2011, through: http://www.hueck-folien.at/index_html?sc=501631312
58. Hulsmann JG. (2008). *"The Ethics of Money Production"*, 1st edition, Ludwig von Mises Institute.
59. Humphrey D. (1993). "Cost and Technical change: Effects from Bank Deregulation", *Journal of Productivity Analysis*, Vol.(4), pp.5-34.
60. KBA-NotaSys. (n.d.). *"KBA-NotaSys"*, Lausanne, Switzerland, accessed on August 29 2011, through http://www.kba-notasys.com/
61. Kmomori. (n.d.). "Banknote and Security Printing Machinery:, accessed on August 29, 2011, through http://www.komori.com/contents_com/product/banknote/index.htm
62. Koeze P. (1982). "The Life-length of Banknote", *Statistica Neer landica*, Vol.36(4), pp.187-207.
63. Koeze P. (1996). "Lecture", June 16-21, *Banknote Printers Conference*, Budapest.
64. Kumbhakar SA. (2000). "Stochastic Frontier Analysis", Cambridge University Press.
65. Lastrapes WD, and Selgin G. (2012). "Banknotes and economic growth", *Scottish Journal of Political Economy*, Vol.59(4), pp.390-418.
66. Lee JK, Jeon SG, and Kim IH. (2004). "Distinctive Point Extraction and Recognition Algorithm for various Kinds of Euro Banknotes", *International Journal of Control, Automation and Systems*, Vol.2(2), pp.201-206.
67. Lieb FW. (2006). *"Life cycle assessment (LCA) of Swiss banknotes"*, December, Swiss National Bank, Cash Division and Environmental Unit, Zurich and Berne.
68. McKinley VA. (2005). *"Central Bank Operational Efficiency: Meaning and Measurement"*, N. C. Nicholl, Ed., Central Banking Publications Ltd., London.

69. Mester L. (2003). "*Applying Efficiency Measurement Techniques to Central Banks*", Federal Reserve Bank of Philadelphia and Finance Department, The Wharton School, University of Pennsylvania.
70. Ministry of Statistics and Programme Implementation. (2011). "*Annual Survey of Industries*", March, Factory Sector 2008-2009, Vol.I, Industrial Statistics Wing, Central Statistics Office, Government of India, Kolkata.
71. Nardo MM. (2005). "Tools for Composite Indicators Building", Institute for the Protection and Security of the Citizen, Ispra, Italy.
72. Nardo M, Saisana M, Saltelli A, Tarantola S, Hoffmann A, and Giovannini E. (2005). "*Handbook on Constructing Composite Indicators: Methodology and User Guide*", OECD, OECD Statistics Working Paper, OECD Publishing, Paris.
73. National Research Council. (1995). "*Currency Features for Visually Impaired People*", Committee on Currency Features Usable by the Visually Impaired, National Academy Press of the National Academy of Sciences, Washington, D.C.
74. National Research Council. (2006). "*Is It Real? Identification and Assessment of the Counterfeiting Threat for U.S. Banknotes*", Committee on Technologies to Deter Currency Counterfeiting, National Academy Press of the National Academy of Sciences, Washington, D.C.
75. National Research Council. (2007). "*A Path to the Next Generation of U.S. Banknotes: Keeping Them Real*", Committee on Technologies to Deter Currency Counterfeiting, National Academy Press of the National Academy of Sciences, Washington, D.C.
76. Note Printing Australia and Securency. (2004). "*Annual report-2004*", Reserve Bank of Australia.
77. Orell Füssli Security Printing Ltd. (2006). "*Banknotes Currency of Noble Origin*", April, Zurich.
78. Papierfabrik Louisenthal GmbH. (n.d.). "*Banknote Paper*", accessed on September 13 2011, through: http://www.louisenthal.com/en/products-and-solutions/banknote-paper/cotton-banknote-paper?section_id=section_15
79. Patel N. (2006). "Development of Printing Business and Role of Accounting", Jabalpur, accessed through http://www.vidyanidhi.org.in/.
80. Pira International. (2011). "*The Future of Banknote Printing to 2016 - Market and Technology*", Publications Department, Pira International, Leatherhead, Surrey.
81. PolyTeQ Services. (2008). "Overcoating Polymer Banknotes the Key to Note Quality, Longer Life & Cleanliness", April, Global Technology Support for Guardian Polymer Substrate, *Banknote Conference*.
82. PolyTeQ Services. (2007). "The Use of Clear Intaglio on Polymer Banknotes", October, Global Technology Support for Guardian Polymer Substrate, *Cross Conference*.
83. Porter EM. (1985). "*Competitive Advantage*", Free Press, New York, USA.
84. Porter EM. (1991). "*The Competitive Advantage of Nations*", Plaza & Janés editors, Barcelona.
85. Porter EM. (1998). "Clusters and the New Economics of Competition", *Harvard Business Review*, Vol.76(7), pp.77-90.
86. Porter M. (1985). "*Competitive Advantage – Creating and Sustaining Superior*", The Free Press, Collier Macmillan Publishers, New York, London.
87. Porter M. (1990). "*The Competitive Advantage of Nations*", Free Press, New York, USA.
88. Prahalad CK. (1990). "The Core Competence of the Corporation", *Harvard Business Review*, Vol.68(3), 79-81.
89. Fare R, Grosskopf S, Norris M, and Zhang Z. (1994). "Productivity Growth, Technical Progress and Efficiency Changes in Industrialised Countries", *American Economic Review*, Vol.84(1), pp.66-83.
90. Raghatate V. (1993). "*A Study of Working Conditions of the Workers in Printing Press Industry in the City of Nagpur 1960-1990*", Nagpur, accessed through: http://www.vidyanidhi.org.in/.
91. Raju KA. (1989). "*Problems and Prospects of Printing Industry: A Case Study of Commercial Presses in Andhra Pradesh*", Waltair, accessed through: http://www.vidyanidhi.org.in/.
92. Razack R. (2002). "*Todywalla Auctions*", November 30, accessed on June 2010, through http://www.todyauction.com/Essays.aspx
93. RBI. (n.d.). "*Frequently Asked Questions*". accessed on August 29 2011, through: http://www.rbi.org.in/currency/faqs.html

94. RBI. (n.d.). *"Security Features"*, accessed on August 29 2011, through: http://www.rbi.org.in/currency/Security%20Features.html
95. Report of the High Level Group. (2009). *"Systems and Procedures for Currency Distribution"*, August, Reserve Bank of India.
96. Research and Markets. (2011). *"A Review of Cotton, Polymer and Multi-Layer Substrates and their Manufactureres"*, June, World Banknote Paper.
97. Reserve Bank of India. (n.d.). *"Security Features"*, accessed on August 29 2011, through: www.rbi.org.in: http://www.rbi.org.in/currency/Security%20Features.html
98. Rivest RL. (1998). *"Perspectives on Financial Cryptography"*, Financial Cryptography, Springer Verlag, Berlin Heidelberg.
99. Sadanand K. (1997). *"Printing in the Telengana Part of the State of Hyderabad"*, Hyderabad, accessed through: http://www.vidyanidhi.org.in/.
100. Saisana MA. (2002). *"State-of-the-art Report on Current Methodologies and Practices for Composite Indicator Development"*, JRC Ispra, Institute for the Protection and Security of the Citizen, Italy.
101. Salzman J. (2003). "Methodological Choices Encountered in the Construction of Composite Indices of Economic and Social Well-Being", Center for the Study of Living Standards, Ontario.
102. Sastane SR. (1988). "Economics of Printing Industry in Pune", Pune, accessed through: http://www.vidyanidhi.org.in/.
103. Seethamma M. (1978). *"Problems of Printing Industry in Madras"*, Pune, accessed through: http://www.vidyanidhi.org.in/.
104. Seiford LA. (1990). "Recent Developments in DEA: The Mathematical Approach to Frontier Analysis", *Journal of Econometrics*, Vol.46, pp.7-38.
105. Sharma S. (2000). "Marketing of Industrial Machinery (With Special Reference to Printing Industry)", February, New Delhi, accessed through: http://www.vidyanidhi.org.in/.
106. Shukla AC. (1975). "Workers' Participationand Industrial Democracy: A Sociological Study of the Workers in Printing Press Industry in Lucknow", Lucknow, accessed through: http://www.vidyanidhi.org.in/.
107. SICPA. (2008). "Creating a Climate of Trust in a World of Uncertainty", 14, World Headquarters, SICPA, 41, Avenue de Florissant, Switzerland.
108. Singh R. (2000). "Employee's Attitude Towards Total Quality Management and Human Resource Development Practices in Printing Industries", Indore, accessed through: http://www.vidyanidhi.org.in/.
109. SPMCIL. (n.d.). accessed on February 12 2010, through: http://cnpnashk.spmcil.com/SPMCIL/interface/History.aspx
110. SPMCIL. (2011). *"FM Receives Maiden Dividend Cheque of Rs.115.43 Crore from SPMCIL"*, August 10, Government of India, Ministry of Finance. Press information Bureau.
111. Sveriges Riks bank. (2005). *"Swedish Banknotes and Coins"*, September, SE-103, Sveriges Riks bank, Stockholm.
112. Swiss National Bank. (2005). *"Technical Aspects of a New Banknote Series"*, February 2, Berne.
113. Symes P. (1993). "Security Features in World Banknotes", August, accessed on 2007, through: http://www.pjsymes.com.au/articles/security.htm
114. Symes P. (1993). accessed on 2009, through: www.pjsymes.com.au/articles/security.htm
115. Tarantola MS. (2002). *"State-of-the-art Report on Current Methodologies and Practices for Composite Indicator Development"*, Institute for the Protection and Security of the Citizen, JRC Ispra, Italy.
116. The Federal Reserve Board. (2005). "New Currency Budget", accessed on July 30 2011, through http://www.federalreserve.gov/generalinfo/foia/2005newcurrency.htm
117. Thrall SL. (1990). "Recent Developments in DEA: The Mathematical Approach to Frontier Analysis", *Journal of Econometrics*, Vol.46, pp.7-38.
118. U.S. Government Printing Office. (1964). *"History of the Bureau of Engraving and Printing 1862-1962"*, Treasury Department, 20402: U.S. Government Printing Office, Washington D. C.

119. Van Renesse RL. (2005). "*Optical Document Security*", Third edition, Artech House Publishers.
120. Velde FR. (1998). "*Lessons from the History of Money*", Economic Perspectives.
121. Wettstein FA. (2006). "*Life cycle assessment (LCA) of Swiss banknotes*", December, Cash Division and Environmental Unit, Swiss National Bank, Berne and Zurich.
122. Wheelen TL, and Hunger JD. (2000). "*Strategic Management and Business Policy – Entering 21st Century Global Society*", 7th edition, Prentice-Hall, New Jersey.
123. Wheelook DA. (1999). "Technical progress, Inefficiency and Productivity Change in U.S. Banking 1984-1993", *Journal of Money, Credit and Banking*, Vol.31(2), pp.212-234.
124. Williams MM, and Anderson RG. (2007). "Currency Design in the United States and Abroad: Counterfeit Deterrence and Visual Accessibility", *Federal Reserve Bank of St. Louis Review*, Vol.89(5), pp.371-414.

www.ingramcontent.com/pod-product-compliance
Lightning Source LLC
Chambersburg PA
CBHW031559210526
45464CB00003B/1344